STRAIGHT TALKING

Alcohol

Sean Connolly

Published by Smart Apple Media
2140 Howard Drive West
North Mankato, MN 56003

Designed by Guy Callaby
Edited by Pip Morgan
Artwork by Karen Donnelly

Photograph acknowledgements

Photographs by Alamy (Boyd, Directphoto.org, Juliet Ferguson,
Medical-on-line, Eric Nathan, Woodystock), Guy Callaby, Getty
Images (AHMAD AL-RUBAYE / AFP, Daniel Allen, ODD ANDERSON /
AFP, Bruce Ayres, Jon Bradley, Lauren Burke, Matt Cardy,
Philip Condit II, Christopher Furlong, Philip Lee Harvey,
PHILIPPE HUGUEN / AFP, The Images Bank, Library of
Congress, MAXIM MARMUR / AFP, Fran May, David
McNew / Newsmakers, Erin Patrice O'Brien, Frank
Siteman, Henrik Sorensen, Justin Sullivan, Mario Tama,
Brunno Vincent, Carsten Witte, David Woolley, David
Young-Wolff), Front cover photograph by Getty Images (Jon Bradley)

Printed in China

Library of Congress
Cataloging-in-Publication Data

Connolly, Sean, 1956-
Alcohol / by Sean Connolly.
p. cm. — (Straight talking)
ISBN-13: 978-1-58340-923-7
1. Alcoholism—Juvenile literature. 2. Children—
Alcohol use—Juvenile literature. 3. Alcoholism—
Prevention—Juvenile literature. I. Title. II. Series.

HV5066.C66 2006
613.81—dc22   2005037707

First Edition

9 8 7 6 5 4 3 2 1

Contents

6
Alcohol and you

8
Alcohol basics

12
Just what happens?

16
Aftereffects

20
Trapped by alcohol

24
Peer pressure

28
Mixed messages

30
Deadly dangers

32
Setting limits

36
School rules

40
Spotting problems

44
Glossary

45
Suggested reading

46
Index

"What's the buzz?" . . . "Where's the buzz?" . . . "I'm buzzing."
These comments are all linked to alcohol and help to give
it an exciting feel—especially for young people. Like other forbidden
activities, drinking alcohol is something people like to talk about
secretly, or to boast about to their friends or others at school.

Alcohol is an
important part
of many people's
lives, particularly
at parties and
other social
events.

Part of a cool crowd

It is not hard to see how you might be tempted to try something, such as
beer, wine, or a wine cooler, that seems to offer a chance for excitement
and wild times—the buzz that many people talk about when describing a
lively party or some crazy prank.

Some people use the word "buzz" to describe the sensation inside
their head when they feel the effects of alcohol or some other drug. To
feel the buzz, to be part of it, to sense it around you—these make you
want to do something. The downside, especially for young people, is that
by not taking part, they will be outsiders or not part of a cool crowd.

> **" Kids who drink are more likely to be victims of violent crime, to be involved in alcohol-related traffic accidents, and to have serious school-related problems. "**

From the Introduction to *Make a Difference: Talk to Your Child About Alcohol*, produced by the United States National Institute on Alcohol Abuse and Alcoholism.

Use and abuse

People in most parts of the world accept that alcohol can play a part in social events, such as weddings and parties. Few find anything wrong with using alcohol for these occasions. Problems develop only when people abuse it: they drink too much, or too often, or when they don't really need it. Then it can become a danger—both to drinkers and to those around them.

Learning to distinguish between use and abuse is an important part of growing up. The results of drinking too much alcohol can be serious, even fatal, but people can learn how to avoid these dangers.

Riot police stand prepared at a soccer game in Europe. Sports rivalries can turn ugly and violent when fans drink too much.

Alcohol is a drug that can change your mood. It is one of the most common mood-altering drugs in the world. Unlike other drugs, such as marijuana or cocaine, it is legal in most countries, even if there are laws to say who can or cannot drink.

Part of our culture

People have been producing wine, beer, and other alcoholic drinks for thousands of years. As a result, alcohol has become part of the culture in many countries—almost a way of life. For example, the English and Americans drink beer, the Scottish drink whiskey, the French and Italians drink wine,

Alcoholic drinks can be part of graveside offerings during Mexico's annual Day of the Dead.

the Russians drink vodka, and the Japanese drink sake (wine made from rice).

Alcohol even plays a part in many religions. Bread and wine are used in many Christian services. Mexicans leave bottles of tequila and beer by the graves of loved ones each year during the Day of the Dead.

Customers at bars and liquor stores can choose from many different alcoholic drinks, which vary widely in alcoholic strength.

An everyday chemical

Most people use the word "alcohol" to refer to the mood-altering ingredient in beer, wine, and other alcoholic drinks. The alcohol in drinks is ethanol alcohol. Ethanol alcohol is produced naturally in a process called fermentation, when sugar is turned into alcohol using yeast. Beer and wine are produced by fermentation, and the alcohol they contain has a proof of around 30. In other words, proof is the strength of the ethanol alcohol in a beverage. Proof is about double the "alcohol by volume" (percent of a drink that is ethanol alcohol) of a drink.

A process called distillation can increase this concentration. Rum, gin, whiskey, and vodka—all produced by distillation—have a proof of about 80 to 85, and sometimes even more.

Ethanol alcohol is only one of a larger group of chemical compounds, all called alcohols, that are used to make varnish, ink, soap, antifreeze, and even explosives. Most are poisonous for humans.

A drawing from the Middle Ages shows people gathering and crushing grapes and collecting the finished wine in a jug.

Drinks through the ages

Wine is probably the oldest alcoholic drink. It is made from grapes, which are are native to the Middle East. The first evidence of people growing grapes to make wine—as opposed to accidentally finding wine—comes from the Caucasus region (where Georgia and Armenia are today). Vineyards existed there between 6,000 and 8,000 years ago.

We know that laborers working on the Egyptian pyramids drank beer and that Egyptian religious ceremonies included wine. Around 500 B.C., the ancient Greeks were producing enough wine to ship to other countries. The Romans followed their example and grew grapes in vineyards throughout their empire, including the modern wine-producing regions of France, Spain, and Italy.

The Arabs were the first people to produce stronger alcoholic drinks using distillation, probably in the 10th century A.D. Europeans were quick to adopt this process. The word "alcohol" comes from an Arabic word meaning "powder," a substance sometimes mixed with distilled alcoholic drinks.

Wine and beer were very popular with Europeans throughout the Middle Ages, partly because distilled drinks, such as whiskey and rum, were expensive to produce.

In the 18th century, new techniques made some distilled drinks, especially gin, less expensive. This caused alarm in London and other major cities. Londoners could get "drunk for a penny and dead drunk for tuppence (two pennies)." The British government added a tax to gin, making it more expensive and less popular. Most governments continue to tax alcoholic drinks—partly to raise money and partly to discourage excessive drinking.

MEASURING ALCOHOL

Measuring alcohol
It is important to know how strong alcoholic drinks are so that people can drink sensibly. The proof is usually shown on the label of bottles and cans of drinks. Alcohol experts use the term serving.

This list shows the proof of common alcoholic drinks:

5-ounce (147 ml) glass of wine, 14–28 proof: **1 serving**

12-ounce (354 ml) bottle of beer, 8–16 proof: **1 serving**

1.5-ounce (44 ml) distilled liquor, 80 proof: **1 serving**

12-ounce (354 ml) wine cooler, 8–16 proof: **1 serving**

The accepted serving amount for men is one to two drinks a day, and one drink a day for women.

This bottle of beer is 12 ounces (354 ml).

www.becks.co.uk
12 oz e
alc. 5% vol.

Alcohol basics | 11

Many people find that alcohol makes them feel happier and less shy when they are socializing in a group.

Most people drink alcohol because they believe it will improve the way they feel. Usually they drink with others—at parties, in a group at a bar, or at someone's house. For these drinkers, alcohol plays an important part in breaking the ice—making them feel more relaxed and sociable. How relaxed people feel, or whether that feeling goes beyond just unwinding, depends on how much they have to drink. It also depends on other factors such as tiredness, their size, and how much they ate before drinking.

People sometimes turn to alcohol because they feel it will make them happier, at least for a while. Lonely, unhappy, or worried people may turn to alcohol as a way to avoid their problems.

Chemical reaction

The changes alcohol triggers come from chemical reactions inside the body. Alcohol passes into the bloodstream through the lining of the small intestine and then affects other parts of the body, especially the brain. Alcohol changes the way the brain operates, including the parts that control concentration, judgment, and body movements. The amount of change depends on how much alcohol reaches the brain.

People can find some of these changes pleasant. For example, after having a drink, someone might feel more able to mingle with strangers at a party. Without alcohol, the brain might have sent the message, "Those people might not find me interesting." Alcohol changes

MORE DANGEROUS

The brain changes during adolescence, and alcohol can seriously harm its growth and development. The frontal lobe (one of the largest regions of the brain), along with many nerve pathways and connections, continues to develop until the age of 16. The brain itself takes another four years to mature. Damage from alcohol at this stage can last a long time, and the brain may never recover. Even moderate drinking affects learning and memory in young people more than in adults.

the brain's way of making judgments—in this case, from being cautious in a group to being more sociable.

Fat and muscle tissue in the body absorb some alcohol before it reaches the brain, so heavy-set or muscular people are often less affected than a thinner person by the same amount of alcohol. Larger people—and more men, compared to women—also have more blood, which can dilute alcohol and lessen its effects.

Many men like to drink large glasses of beer.

Binge drinkers go through a lot of alcohol—or drink very quickly—in order to feel the effects of being drunk.

BINGE DRINKING

People become very drunk when the alcohol in their blood—the blood alcohol level—increases before the body can process the alcohol already there. It takes several hours for the effects of a single drink (such as a beer or a glass of wine) to wear off, so having several drinks usually leads to drunkenness.

Most responsible drinkers pace themselves so this does not happen. Others deliberately drink large amounts over a short time to get drunk. Young people—even those old enough to drink legally—risk injuring themselves or others with this behavior, which is called binge drinking. Alcohol awareness organizations are concerned that advertising aimed at young people makes drinking seem necessary for having a good time.

EFFECTS OF ALCOHOL

These are the progressive effects of becoming drunk (intoxication). People go through these stages if they continue drinking alcohol without allowing enough time for the effects to wear off.

Stage 1
People become more confident, comfortable, and talkative.

Stage 2
People's thinking becomes less clear, and they will probably say things they are likely to regret.

Stage 3
They become unsteady and confused, with slurred speech. They might behave unpredictably and become violent.

Stage 4
Drinkers are very confused and find it hard to stand. At this stage, many drinkers pass out (become unconscious).

Stage 5
People who remain conscious and continue drinking are in grave danger. Their nervous system has trouble working; they could stop breathing and even die.

During celebrations fueled by alcohol, some students at Oxford University in the United Kingdom (UK) jump off of bridges into the river.

" *I don't particularly worry about the negative physical effects—not yet, anyway. In spite of the drinking and smoking, I'm reasonably healthy, and at my last checkup (five years ago, admittedly) my liver was fine. If I have a hangover, I'm fairly tolerant of it. However, the psychological effects do worry me. I can take an aspirin for a headache, but the only thing I can take for the anxiety and depression that follows heavy drinking is . . . another drink, of course.* "

Joe, a musician and gardener.

SOBERING MYTHS

A number of myths surround the issue of drinking and sobering up afterwards. Many people believe that drinking coffee helps to speed up the sobering process because it contains the stimulant caffeine. Others say that taking a cold shower or walking it off can help someone become sober more quickly. None of these actions actually help get rid of the effects of alcohol. The body does this at its own pace. Such misconceptions are risky if someone is drunk enough to be a dangerous driver. Alcohol also affects judgment, so a drinker can easily believe these myths and convince others that he or she is safe behind the wheel.

A COMMUNITY ROAD SAFETY PROJECT

Know your limits - DRIVE SOBER

Drinking alcohol, especially regularly over a long period of time, can have more effects than simply making someone happy, or even very drunk. Some effects are felt after the first time someone drinks alcohol. Most regular drinkers can describe the awful feeling of a hangover (see page 18). Alcohol also works over time and can lead to serious medical conditions if a person drinks heavily for several years, or longer.

A sign beside a highway urges motorists to think carefully about drinking and driving.

Going beyond the limit

All of these effects arise because alcohol is a drug that affects the body. Too much of any drug can damage the body and the way it operates. That is why presciption drugs have clear instructions on how much to take and what to do if someone has a bad reaction. Sensible drinkers know that alcohol has safe limits. Going beyond these, especially time after time, is very dangerous.

Besides a headache, many people with hangovers have an upset stomach because alcohol affects the digestive system. A hangover usually wears off after a few hours, although some drinkers have another alcoholic drink to relieve the pain. This just postpones the hangover, which is usually worse later. Needing a drink in the morning is a sign that a person might be dependent on alcohol (see pages 20–23).

LONG-TERM EFFECTS

Alcohol reaches most parts of the body through the bloodstream. Getting drunk and feeling sick because of a hangover are some of the short-term effects of having alcohol in the body. But regular drinking over time can have damaging—even fatal—consequences. Below are some parts of the body that can be affected by long-term drinking, no matter how young the drinker is.

1 Liver The liver can only absorb alcohol slowly. Too much alcohol damages liver cells, leading to diseases such as cirrhosis and cancer.

2 Stomach Alcohol can make people very sick and can cause ulcers and other stomach problems.

3 Heart Alcohol can make the heart work much harder than normal. This stress can lead to high blood pressure and heart disease.

4 Brain Alcohol kills brain cells and depresses the central nervous system. It has a bad effect on concentration, balance, coordination, reflexes, vision, and judgment.

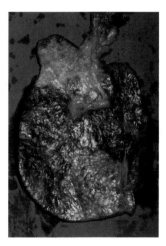

This photograph shows how the normally smooth wall of the liver becomes damaged and scarred by cirrhosis.

> **" I think that awareness of alcohol poisoning should be higher. I am a high honor student with a part-time job. I am smart. I got so drunk last month that I passed out downtown, almost died, and got taken to the hospital. "**

Seventeen-year-old boy.

THE SOCIAL COST

Alcohol damages society as a whole, contributing to or causing a wide range of crimes. The National Council on Alcoholism and Drug Dependence has gathered some alarming statistics from government reports in the U.S. The facts and figures paint a worrisome picture of the role of alcohol in society.

● *Each year, there are reports of three million violent crimes in which the attacker was under the influence of alcohol.*

● *Attackers in violent crimes are more likely to be under the influence of alcohol than of any other drug.*

● *About two-thirds of violent incidents between couples take place when one of them has been drinking.*

● *About 70 percent of violent incidents involving alcohol use occur in the home.*

American police officers test the ability of a suspected drunk driver to walk in a straight line without losing his balance.

THE MORNING AFTER

One of the first unpleasant side effects of drinking alcohol is a hangover. Among other things, alcohol takes moisture from the body's cells, including the brain. This dryness leads to headaches and an uncomfortable reaction to sudden noises. People usually feel the effects of a hangover after the immediate effects of drinking alcohol have worn off—often when they wake up the next morning.

SEARCHING QUESTION

Health insurance companies pay for most expensive medical treatments. Some patients need treatment because they have drunk too much alcohol. Is it right that others should pay for treatment that might not have been necessary if the patient had not abused alcohol for so long?

Dependence on alcohol can lead a person to drink alone and to lose self-respect.

Drinking alcohol, like taking other drugs, can become a habit that is hard to break. People with alcohol dependence, or alcoholism, find it almost impossible to stop drinking. They have one drink, then another, and continue drinking until they pass out or fall asleep. Then, waking up with a terrible hangover, they start drinking again.

The disease of alcoholism

For years, many thought alcoholism was a shameful problem suffered by people who had no willpower. Because of this, friends and relatives tried to hide the person's drinking from others. Nowadays, doctors consider alcoholism to be a disease, linked to a person's psychological and physical dependence on alcohol.

Exactly what causes alcoholism is still a mystery, but some people are more likely to develop it than others. Medical studies show that some families have a history of alcohol problems. This suggests that alcoholism might be linked to a person's genes.

Facing facts

Even though alcoholism is considered a disease, people should not continue to drink heavily and wait for treatment if the disease develops. Many people with alcoholism do not realize or accept that they have a problem; they think alcoholism is something that affects other people. They forget that the disease develops slowly. If they or their friends do not recognize some of the warning signs (see panel), alcoholism can become very serious.

Alcohol becomes a way of life for people with a serious dependence. They plan their day around drinking, ignoring or forgetting about their other activities and responsibilities. If they continue drinking, they risk losing their job, failing at school, or wrecking their relationships. They may also become aggressive and violent.

Alcohol dependence can develop in people of all ages. Teenagers, as well as adults, can become dependent on alcohol.

Fans still lay tributes at the Paris grave of American rock star Jim Morrison, who died in 1971 after many years of heavy drinking.

WARNING SIGNS

Alcoholism takes time to develop, but a number of signs warn that a drinking problem could develop into alcohol dependence, or alcoholism. The U.S. National Institute on Alcohol Abuse and Alcoholism lists these for young people. On their own, most signs would be thought normal for adolescents. However, a combination of signs—or if any occur suddenly or violently—might be a clue to the real problem.

● *Mood changes: occurrences of temper and irritability.*

● *School problems: bad grades, poor attendance, or getting into trouble.*

● *Rebelling against family rules.*

● *Changing friends and not introducing new friends to the family.*

● *A "nothing matters" attitude: sloppy appearance, a lack of involvement in former interests, and low energy.*

● *Physical or mental problems: memory lapses, poor concentration, bloodshot eyes, lack of coordination, or slurred speech.*

" Basically, taking a flask and that sort of thing to school to get through the day and just to deal with life. It sort of became a social dependence I guess. Yeah, drinking half a bottle of whiskey just to get through each day. . . . At boarding school, . . . in the house, in class. I've always had a problem with anything I've enjoyed. I always go all out, and when I found alcohol and I enjoyed it, yeah, I did go all out. I drank as much as I could get my hands on whenever I could. **"**

A teenager describing how his alcohol dependence began at the age of 12.

Some heavy drinkers, including young people, find themselves out of work and homeless because of their problems with alcohol.

ALCOHOL WITHDRAWAL SYNDROME

The sight of an addict suffering because he or she is quitting a drug is very disturbing. Someone who is dependent on heroin goes through a very uncomfortable period called "cold turkey," when the body experiences withdrawal symptoms. Alcohol dependency also leads to unpleasant experiences when the drinker goes without alcohol; in some ways, these symptoms are more serious than those linked to heroin.

The medical name for these symptoms is *delirium tremens*, although many people call this Alcohol Withdrawal Syndrome. *Delirium tremens* is a Latin phrase, meaning "trembling delirium." It describes the uncontrolled shaking a person experiences, often accompanied by vivid hallucinations. Alcohol Withdrawal Syndrome is very exhausting, leaving the person drained and terrified. People suffering from this condition should have emergency medical care—even then, the withdrawal symptoms might be fatal.

Some teenagers think that if they drink—and smoke cigarettes—they will look cool and mature.

Studies from around the world agree that alcohol is by far the most popular drug used by young people. In the U.S., for example, it is used more than all illegal drugs combined. Using alcohol is illegal for young people, yet alcohol is sold openly to those old enough to drink it legally. It is almost impossible to prevent some older people from buying it for, or even selling it to, underage drinkers.

Italy may be one of the world's leading wine producers, but many Italian teenagers avoid drinking alcohol when they are having fun.

Alcohol use among young people has been rising in many countries for decades, and it continues to rise. Although schools, youth groups, and even alcohol producers have highlighted the risks, the problem is increasing. Why?

The power of persuasion

One of the most powerful forces attracting young people to alcohol—and to other illegal drugs—is peer pressure. Many people feel embarrassed or ashamed to be left out of a new, dangerous activity. Young people often begin drinking because they believe it will give them a cool image. The teen years are a time for learning how to accept responsibilities and to make sensible judgments. Many teenagers find it hard to refuse alcohol, and if they do begin drinking, they lack the experience to function when alcohol clouds their judgment.

The results can be tragic. In 2001, the U.S. National Highway Traffic Safety Administration reported that 3,594 youths between the ages of 15 and 20 were killed in car crashes in which someone had been drinking. Police test for alcohol at traffic accidents, but there are many other types of fatal accidents in which alcohol is involved. Many children die from these other alcohol-related causes: drowning, burning, suicide, and alcohol poisoning.

ALCOHOL FACT

One survey found that more than a quarter of boys ages 9 to 10 and a third of those a year older reported drinking alcohol at least once in the previous week, usually at home.

" *In our city, teens drink for one reason: there is nothing else to do. It's like it's their only way to have some fun. Every city should take care of their young people as much as possible by offering them more activities.* **"**

Seventeen-year-old boy.

A Scottish youth holds two bottles of wine as he poses for a passing photographer.

Changing times

The UK Office for National Statistics has followed trends in drinking alcohol and other activities for many decades. Its findings show that alcohol use has increased dramatically among young people. Before 1950, people ages 18 to 24 drank less alcohol than any other adult age group in Britain. During the 1950s, teenagers began drinking, but most gathered in coffee houses rather than bars. It was only in the 1960s that young people began going to bars regularly, signaling a sudden rise in alcohol use. By the 1980s, the 18 to 24 age group had reversed its position of 30 years earlier—it had become the adult group that drank the most alcohol.

Champagne is part of the popular image of young women who attend the races at Ascot in England.

SEARCHING QUESTION

Imagine you have just arrived at a party where most of the young people, including some of your friends, are drinking. They urge you to join them, but you don't want to drink any alcohol. Can you think of a way to refuse their offer without making them—or you—feel embarrassed?

Eye-catching labels make bottles of wine coolers look like soda pop on the shelves in stores.

Even secure young people can find the issue of alcohol complicated. On one hand, adults warn about the serious problems relating to alcohol. On the other hand, advertisements and TV commercials show people having a great time with alcohol. What's true, and how can young people make up their minds?

Controlling advertisements

Learning to decode the mixed messages we receive from society is an important part of growing up. Most adults can make up their minds without too much persuasion from friends or from the world of advertising. Younger people have had less experience, though, and find these decisions harder to make.

As a result, most countries have strict guidelines about how alcohol can be advertised. In some countries, such as the U.S., a TV commercial cannot show people putting a glass or bottle of alcohol to their lips. In the UK, there are fewer restrictions. A commercial cannot show drinking alcohol as the only reason a group of people is having a good time. Nearly everywhere, alcohol advertising is forbidden in magazines for young people and on TV during the day when young people are most likely to be watching.

ALCOHOL FACT

In the U.S., middle and high school students drink 35 percent of all wine coolers and 1.1 billion cans of beer.

From *Youth and Alcohol: A National Survey. Drinking Habits, Access, Attitudes, and Knowledge,* Washington, D.C., June 1991.

Targeting young drinkers

Wine coolers mask the taste of alcohol with sweet or fruity flavors. It is very easy to drink several without realizing their strength. They are often far stronger than beer.

The youth advertising message is effective, even on those who are too young to drink alcohol legally. A U.S. survey found that eighth-grade students were as likely to drink wine coolers as beer. A similar survey in Wales found that parents were giving children wine coolers at parties.

➡️ *Student bars are popular meeting places for young people in college.*

SEARCHING QUESTION

Many parents, police officers, and alcohol counselors worry that advertising alcoholic drinks encourages people—especially young people—to drink too much early in their lives. Some would like to see alcohol advertising controlled more strictly or even banned. What do you think?

A police officer uses a Breathalyzer to measure the amount of alcohol in a driver's body.

Imagine how frightening it would be to face a drunk person waving a deadly weapon. When someone who has had too much to drink drives a car, he or she turns it into a lethal weapon. Even at very low speeds, a car can severely injure or kill people—pedestrians or passengers. That possibility makes driving a big responsibility. Drivers need to make split-second decisions. Even the smallest amount of alcohol in the blood can affect a person's driving ability.

Drunk people often become loud and violent and occasionally have deadly weapons. Others, especially young people who have adolescent troubles, can feel overwhelmed by their worries and harm themselves. Alcohol makes them forget how to address these anxieties with common sense. This can be dangerous for young drinkers and for those around them.

SAFETY TIPS

The U.S. activist group Mothers Against Drunk Driving (MADD) publicizes the dangers of drinking alcohol and driving. Often, children cannot refuse a ride from an adult (sometimes a loved one) who has had too much alcohol to drive a car safely. The organization offers children the following advice, which could save a life.

ALWAYS:
Sit in the back seat.

Buckle up tight.

Put all items on the floor.

Don't bother the driver—just sit quietly.

Tell a trusted grown-up about any dangerous ride.

Deadly combination

People who have drunk alcohol lose coordination and take dangerous risks—a deadly combination. In July 2000, a team of Swedish doctors published the results of a five-year survey of the link between alcohol and accidental deaths. They found that 29 percent of all accidental deaths in Sweden were linked to alcohol and estimated that the figure could be as high as 44 percent in countries such as the UK and Australia, where the laws are less strict.

These results are supported by alcohol experts in other countries. The National Strategy for Suicide Prevention in the U.S. reports that alcohol plays a part in 40 to 60 percent of U.S. suicides. According to Alcohol Concern, 8 out of 10 people treated in emergency rooms in the UK at peak times have had an accident linked to alcohol.

A bunch of flowers marks the site of a fatal car accident.

Iraqi men drink
tea at a café.
Most Iraqis
belong to the
Islamic faith,
which bans the
use of alcohol.

For thousands of years, families, schools, religious groups, and countries have tried to set limits on the use and availability of alcohol. Some limits are aimed at a particular group, mainly the young, who risk the most by drinking. Other limits have been designed to stop everyone from drinking because of the problems alcohol can cause society as a whole.

Underage drinking

Some Islamic countries, such as Saudi Arabia, ban alcohol completely because it is against their religion. Most countries set strict limits for young people to prevent underage drinking. Australians under 18 cannot buy or drink alcohol legally.

In the UK, the 1964 Licensing Act gives more detailed guidelines. People under 14 cannot enter most bars. Those who are 16 and over can have low-proof alcoholic drinks, such as beer, with a meal in a bar or restaurant, provided they are with an adult. Otherwise, the law is the same as in Australia.

The U.S. has changed its drinking laws many times. Until 1984, each state decided its own laws. Then, the federal government passed the National Minimum Drinking Age Act, which required all states to raise the age for buying and drinking alcohol to 21.

An underage drinker hides his alcohol in a paper bag. Without guidance, young people find it hard to know their drinking limits.

SEARCHING QUESTION

Many people believe that tough punishments act as a deterrent. In other words, knowing that the punishment for an action will be severe, a person will probably choose not to do it. Many people believe that the punishments for drunk driving are not serious enough to be a deterrent. Can you think of a punishment that would stop more people from starting a car after they have had a drink?

Young Italians first taste wine at family gatherings, and most of them remain sensible drinkers.

GOING EASY IN ITALY

Italians drink roughly the same amount of alcohol per person as people in countries such as the UK and the U.S., but Italy has fewer social problems linked to alcohol—such as violence and public drunkenness. Italians are brought up drinking wine and other alcoholic beverages. This means that most of them have their first drink in a family setting, where they learn about the dangers of drinking. As a result, teenagers consider alcohol as just one of the things that goes with meeting other people—never the only reason for people to get together.

Young and old Italians frown on drinking too much, especially in public. Dr. Enrico Tempesta, an Italian government scientist studying alcohol and youth, explains: "Here, children and teenagers disapprove of and tend to exclude from their circle a contemporary who gets drunk."

Police officers destroy barrels of rum in San Francisco during Prohibition, the period during which the U.S. banned all alcoholic drinks.

Banning alcohol

Around the middle of the 19th century, many Americans—especially women—were concerned about alcohol and its effects on the country. Many men regularly went to saloons, spent their wages on drinks, and often left their families with little money to live. Drinking also affected the economy, with many people missing work, arriving late, or trying to work while drunk.

By the beginning of the 20th century, groups favoring prohibition (banning alcohol altogether) in the U.S. gained support. Similar movements developed in Canada, Finland, and the UK. In 1919, the U.S. government amended, or changed, the Constitution so that alcohol was banned across the country. Prohibition remained in effect throughout the 1920s, though many Americans found ways of drinking alcohol in speakeasies (secret bars) or through bootleggers (people who imported alcohol illegally).

By the early 1930s, many Americans had tired of Prohibition and believed that individuals, not the government, should be allowed to decide for themselves whether or not to drink alcohol. In 1933, the Constitution was changed again, making it legal once more to sell, buy, and drink alcohol in the U.S.

SEARCHING QUESTION

Some Americans argue that the drinking age should be lowered in the U.S. But some experts in the UK and other countries want to raise their drinking age to 21. What do you think?

↑
Teenage drinking can lead to tiredness and poor performance at school.

Teachers and others in the education system need to have a common policy on how to keep their schools free of alcohol and ensure that alcohol drunk off school grounds does not disrupt other children's chances to learn.

In nearly every country, school-age children are too young to drink alcohol legally, but calling the police into school every time a child is suspected of drinking would be very disruptive. Like parents, school staff members have a duty to look after young people. That duty sometimes calls for a delicate balance—disciplining drinkers, while at the same time offering positive alternatives to having alcohol.

Zero tolerance

One of the most dramatic ways of dealing with alcohol in schools is to be very strict once the school rules about drinking alcohol have been broken.

Many schools in the U.S. and other countries operate a zero-tolerance policy toward alcohol. Students know that they won't simply receive a warning the first time they are caught—they will face a severe penalty imposed by the school, which could be expulsion.

People in favor of zero-tolerance policies believe that schools benefit from children understanding the severe consequences they face when they drink illegally.

Students at West Covina High School in Los Angeles carry a coffin into the school gym. This is part of a course that teaches teens that someone is killed in an alcohol-related car crash every 15 minutes. The students role-play the deaths of four teenagers in the space of an hour. They write obituaries and reenact failed attempts to save the teenagers' lives.

Targeting the source

There would be no alcohol problem in any school if underage people could not obtain alcohol. But many young people who drink have been able to buy alcohol.

A UK survey in 2000 found that 63 percent of 16- to 17-year-olds and 10 percent of 12- to 15-year-olds who had drunk in the previous year usually bought their own alcohol. Most bought drinks in bars and clubs. Only a third of the underage drinkers who tried to buy alcohol had been turned down.

A plan was launched in 2004 to tackle this problem. The UK Home Office targeted more than 1,800 bars, clubs, and liquor stores. More than half of the bars and clubs, and just under a third of liquor stores, were selling alcohol to minors. These operations—and heavy fines for those who sell to underage people—should help schools deal with the problem of school-age drinking.

> ❝ **Some students come into school drunk or with hangovers. It has quite a devastating effect. They come into school with a hangover, they've got a headache, they want to sleep, they can't concentrate. . . . It sometimes leads to behavior that has a horrible effect on the rest of the group, and their learning is affected.** ❞

A school principal, recorded in a BBC News Survey, 2004.

EFFECTS ON LEARNING

Schools take a tough stand on alcohol. Classes on alcohol and other drugs help students understand the consequences of drinking. Teachers and counselors are trained to look for warning signs and to give candid advice about alcohol to students.

Students who drink also affect the school's overall performance. Medical problems, bad behavior, and aggression disrupt the learning process for other students. So schools need to protect others from the effects of the few who drink.

Like more and more teenagers in the world, these Russian girls illegally drink beer in a Moscow park.

SEARCHING QUESTION
Some people argue that a zero-tolerance approach to alcohol and drugs is unfair because it does not give students a chance to improve their behavior. Also, children might be wrongly accused or set up by fellow students. Do you think these concerns are enough to stop such policies, or do you think schools need firm punishments when dealing with alcohol and other substances?

Someone who has a problem with alcohol may feel very lonely. That problem can come from drinking, or from the sadness and stress of having a family member who drinks too much. A good way to approach the issue is to talk to someone. Young people who feel comfortable at home should turn to older family members.

Looking for advice

Beyond the family, many individuals and groups can offer help and advice. Schools and youth groups can point a young person in the direction of trained counselors who are experts in helping people of all ages come to terms with alcohol.

Some national and international alcohol organizations are listed at the end of this book, along with some recommended books on the subject. More local organizations are listed in the telephone book under the headings "alcohol," "alcohol awareness," and "alcohol concerns." Type in similar phrases, along with the nearest town or city, to search the Internet for Web sites and addresses of organizations.

Many young people find it easier to deal with their alcohol problems in discussion groups or counseling sessions.

Family matters

Problems with drinking by young people spill over into families—causing arguments and endangering relationships between parents and children, and brothers and sisters. Sometimes problems can be traced back to the parents. Their attitudes and habits relating to alcohol shape much of their children's behavior.

Parents with alcohol problems make their children suffer. Many children often do poorly in school and have emotional and psychological problems. These children may find it hard to move into adulthood and keep friendships, and may pull away from family members. Some begin drinking heavily, creating problems for the next generation.

AN INSIDER'S STORY

Jenny (not her real name) is 18. Her story is typical of people who don't realize they have a serious drinking problem.

"I started drinking beer when I was 14. Older friends would buy me and my friends a few cans or bottles. We'd spend Friday and Saturday evening drinking, either at the far end of the park or at someone's house if their parents were out. It was fun at first, but then I started to feel like I wanted to drink more, and more often."

Shoplifting

"I would tell my parents that I was at a sleepover or party and then start drinking at lunchtime on Saturday. Then I began to skip school and hang out with some older kids who also liked to drink. Sometimes I shoplifted alcohol if I had no money. Other times, I would go into the bar with the older kids—only if it was crowded and the staff didn't notice me. I started to have real problems at school, and most of my older friends—even the ones I had started drinking with—ignored me. At that time, I thought, 'No way do I have a drinking problem. It's not vodka or even wine—just beer and maybe a wine cooler.'"

> **" I would tell my parents that I was at a sleepover or party and then start drinking at lunchtime on Saturday. "**

Getting help

"The principal at my school finally cornered me. She told me to face the facts—not aggressively or threatening me. Just to face the facts and see where my life was leading. I argued a bit, trying to defend myself, but eventually I got the nerve to phone an alcohol advisory center. They were great—no hassle, just good at listening. I started coming over to talk, and they showed me how I'd start to enjoy life much more if I stayed sober. That came as a shock. 'What, me? An alcoholic?' I thought. But it was worth listening. I took their advice and have stopped drinking. I even told some of my older friends about it, right after I made my decision. They were great, and they've been really supportive of me over the first few months. I've even joined a drama group—it helps me let off steam if I feel frustrated."

> **" The principal at my school cornered me. She told me to face the facts. "**

Young people can laugh, share secrets, and have a good time without needing to drink alcohol.

adolescence the period in a person's teenage years marking the change from child to adult

alcohol poisoning an overdose of alcohol that puts physical stress on one or more parts of the body

alcoholism a physical and psychological dependence on alcohol

binge drinking drinking a large amount of alcohol at one time

blitz a sudden attack

bloodshot (eyes) appearing red and showing small blood vessels

cirrhosis an alcohol-related disease of the liver caused by a build-up of scar tissue

compound a chemical mixture of two or more substances

concentration the amount of a particular substance found in a mixture

constitution a written document spelling out how a country is governed

contemporary a person about the same age as yourself

culture the customs and way of life of a country

dilute to add another substance to a mixture (usually a liquid) to lessen the concentration of something else

distillation a process of producing strong alcoholic drinks by boiling a liquid that contains alcohol to rid it of other ingredients

fatal causing death

fermentation a natural way of producing alcoholic drinks (such as wine) by leaving a juice so that its sugar turns into alcohol

genes the basic chemical code of human beings, which determines how they will develop

hallucination an imaginary vision caused by a high fever or a drug

hangover an unpleasant feeling, including dry mouth, headache, and upset stomach, experienced the day after drinking a lot of alcohol

high blood pressure a medical condition in which a person's blood pressure is persistently higher than normal

HIV/AIDS HIV is an abbreviation for human immunodeficiency virus, which can cause a deadly condition called acquired immune deficiency syndrome (AIDS)

import to bring in from another country

insecure lacking in confidence

insurance a type of payment that provides money in an accident or emergency

Islamic relating to the Muslim religion, based on the teachings of the Prophet Muhammad

licensing giving legal permission to sell a product such as alcohol

peer pressure powerful persuasion from friends to do something

prescription drugs medicines that a doctor decides are necessary to treat an illness

prohibition a ban on a particular action (from the word "prohibit," or forbid)

proof the strength of alcohol in a beverage; the higher the number, the stronger the drink

psychological having to do with the mind

reaction a chemical change

sexually transmitted disease an illness passed on from one person to another through sexual activity

stimulant a drug that makes people feel more alert

ulcer a hole in the stomach lining

vineyard an area where grape vines are grown

withdrawal symptoms the physical and psychological changes in a person who stops taking a drug after becoming dependent on it

Books

Bennett, Trevor. *Understanding Drugs, Alcohol, and Crime.* New York: Open University Press, 2005.

Center for Substance Abuse Prevention (U.S.). *Tips for Teens: the Truth About Alcohol.* Rockville, Md.: U.S. Department of Health and Human Services, 2004.

Crist, James J. *When Someone You Love Abuses Alcohol or Drugs—A Guide for Kids.* Stevens Point, Wis.: Wellness Institute, 2003.

Dudley, William. *Alcohol.* San Diego: Greenhaven Press, 2001.

Gottfried, Ted. *The Facts About Alcohol.* New York: Benchmark Books, 2005.

MacLachlan, Malcolm. *Binge Drinking and Youth Culture.* Dublin: Liffey Press, 2004.

Web sites

Al-Anon and Alateen
www.Al-Anon-Alateen.org
Offers advice and practical steps for young people whose families or friends are affected by alcohol abuse.

AlcoholismResources.com
alcoholismresources.com/teens_alcohol_tips.htm
Offers information about alcohol, its effects, and how to recognize the signs that someone you know has an alcohol problem.

Check Yourself
www.checkyourself.com/Resources.aspx
Provides facts for those who have questions about alcohol and other drugs, along with information on treatment centers and alcohol hotlines.

The Cool Spot
www.thecoolspot.org
A Web site aimed at young people's concerns about alcohol, with interactive quizzes, polls, and information about alcohol and how to say no to peer pressure.

MADD
www.madd.org/under21/1107
The Web site of Mothers Against Drunk Driving offers several resources about teenage drinking, including facts, myths, and activities.

Talk4Teens
www.talk4teens.co.uk
A Web site covering the most important teen health issues, including a detailed and useful section on alcohol.

Index

accidents 7, 25, 31
addicts 23
advertising 13, 28, 29
aftereffects 16, 17
AIDS 31
alcohol abuse 7
alcohol poisoning 17, 25
Alcohol Withdrawal
   Syndrome 23
alcoholism 20, 21
anxiety 15, 30
Arabs 11

balance 17, 18
bars 9, 12, 27, 32, 38
beer 6, 8, 9, 11, 13, 29,
   32, 39
binge drinking 13
blood pressure 17
bloodstream 12, 17
bootleggers 35
brain 12, 13, 17

caffeine 13
cancer 17
champagne 27
chemicals 9, 12
cigarettes 24
cirrhosis 17
cocaine 8
coffee 13
cold turkey 23
concentration 12, 17, 21,
   39
coordination 17, 21, 31
counselors 39, 40
crime 7, 18

deaths 25, 31
delirium tremens 23
depression 15, 31
distillation 9, 11
driving 15, 25, 29, 30, 33,
   37
drowning 25

drugs 8, 20, 23, 24, 31, 39

Egyptians 11
ethanol 9
ethyl alcohol 9

fermentation 9
figures 18, 25, 27, 33

genes 20
gin 9, 11
grapes 11
Greeks 11

hallucinations 23
hangovers 15, 16, 18, 20,
   39
headaches 15, 16, 39
heart 17
heroin 23
HIV 31
homelessness 22
hospital 17

intestines 12

judgment 12, 13, 15, 17,
   25, 31

laws 8, 31, 32, 33, 35
liquor store 9, 38
liver 15, 17
loneliness 12, 40

marijuana 8
measures 11
medical treatment 19
medicines 16
memory 21
moods 21
myths 15, 29

organizations 13, 40, 45

parties 6, 7, 12, 27, 29

peer pressure 25
Prohibition 35
proof 9, 11
punishments 33

reflexes 17
religions 9, 32
Romans 11

sake 8
school 6, 7, 21, 22, 25, 29,
   32, 36, 37, 39, 41, 42,
   43
servings 11
sex 31
smoking 24
speakeasies 35
sports 7
stomach 16, 17
stress 31, 40
suicide 25, 31

tax 11
tequila 9
TV 28

ulcers 17

vineyards 11
violence 18, 34
vision 17
vodka 8, 9, 11, 42

warning signs 21
weddings 7
whiskey 8, 9, 11, 22, 29
wine 6, 8, 9, 11, 13, 25,
   26, 29, 34, 42
wine cooler 6, 11, 28, 29,
   42

zero tolerance 37, 39